Praise for

The Power of Sacred Space . . .

"Carolyn Cobelo has discovered the Holy Grail where we least expect it—in sacred places around the world! Reading her amazing insights is like having a personal guide to hidden spiritual realities of which few civilized people are aware. . . . *The Power of Sacred Space* is itself a talisman—a magical object charged with spiritual power to heal and evolve those who touch it."

—Dennis William Hauck
Author of *Haunted Places* and
The Emerald Tablet: Alchemy for Personal Transformation

"*The Power of Sacred Space* takes us into the core of our heritage, where we can avail ourselves of hidden wisdom. It offers many useful facts, yet the most insightful gems are to be found in the author's own channeling of the spirits of places she describes. Carolyn Cobelo gives us the tools and the *permission* to hear the essence of each sacred space and to bring it to life in our own hearts."

—Diego Mulligan
Anchor for *The Journey Home Radio Show*

Also by Carolyn E. Cobelo

Avalon: The Temple of Connection

The Spring of Hope: Messages from Mary

Awakening to Soul Love: Pathways to Intimacy

Twenty-Five Power Places: A Travel Guide

THE POWER OF SACRED SPACE

Exploring Ancient Ceremonial Sites

Carolyn E. Cobelo

Akasha Productions
Santa Fe, New Mexico

Published by:
Akasha Productions
223 N. Guadalupe, Suite 402
Santa Fe, New Mexico 87505

Editor: Ellen Kleiner
Book design and production: Marilyn Hager
Cover design and production: Janine Lehmann
Back cover photo: Jennifer Esperanza

A Blessingway Book

Copyright © 2000 by Carolyn E. Cobelo

All rights reserved. No part of this book may be reproduced
by any means or in any form whatsoever without written
permission from the publisher, except for brief quotations
embodied in literary articles and reviews.

Printed in the United States of America

Publisher's Cataloging-in-Publication Data

Cobelo, Carolyn E.
  The power of sacred space : exploring ancient ceremonial sites /
  by Carolyn E. Cobelo. -- 1st ed.
  p.cm.
  LCCN: 99-72135
  ISBN: 0-9670412-3-6

  1. Sacred space. 2. Sacred space--Guidebooks. 3. Shrines.
  4. Earth--Religious aspects. 5. Spiritual life--New Age
  movement. I. Title.

BL580.C63 2000   291.3'5
                                                         QBI99-759

10 9 8 7 6 5 4 3 2 1

To Esteban E. Cobelo—
my guide and protector on our journeys
to sacred places

ACKNOWLEDGMENTS

I would first like to acknowledge and thank Esteban E. Cobelo, who is now in spirit, for his guidance, protection, and companionship on our many journeys in this world.

I would also like to thank my children, Nicole, Tonya, and Sophie, as well as my parents, Ruth and James Ewing, and my Cobelo family in Buenos Aires, Argentina, for their patience, support, and understanding while I researched this book.

Thanks, too, to the students of Akasha Institute in New York and Buenos Aires for their trust and their support of my leadership during our pilgrimages to some of these sacred sites.

Special thanks to Marilyn Hager for her beautiful graphic design of this book and to Ellen Kleiner for her excellent editing.

My deepest gratitude goes out to the spirits of all the sacred places I visited, for their receptivity, communication, and wisdom.

Contents

Illustrations

INTRODUCTION

Sacred space is a place where we honor the divine in its material form. The purpose of sacred space is to awaken an awareness of our intimate connection to the spiritual world and to the universe as a whole.

This guidebook is designed to enrich and deepen your experience of sacred space. If you take it with you when you visit ancient sites, it will help you connect to the energy and the spirits there. It can also be used to create a sacred space of your own in your home or office.

The primary source for this book is the intuitive knowledge that emerged as I traversed the Earth in search of the wisdom of sacred space. Over seven years of following spiritual guidance, I was led to places in the Middle East, North America, South America, and Europe. I traveled alone; with my husband Esteban, who is now in spirit; and as a group leader on spiritual pilgrimages. Everywhere, the information that surfaced shared a common perspective and focus.

For purposes of this book, the information has been arranged in a sequence that leads from the macrocosmic to the microcosmic, from what exists in faraway cultures to what you can "bring home" to a corner of your living or work space. Chapter 1 defines the special aspects of sacred space. Chapter 2 provides insight into the spiritual effects of sacred space. Chapter 3 contains transcripts of messages received at sacred sites. Chapter 4 offers guidance in attuning to sacred space. Chapter 5 demonstrates the capacity of sacred space to accelerate personal spiritual evolution.

Chapter 6 describes how sacred space replicates the order of the universe. Chapter 7 discusses various forms of sacred geometry found at sacred sites. Chapter 8 gives guidelines for creating sacred space in your home or office, and for keeping it sacred. Chapter 9 presents an exercise for communicating with the spirits of a sacred space.

Enjoy!

Chapter 1

THE IMPORTANCE OF SACRED SPACE

Sacred space offers us a profound vehicle for personal and global healing, and an endless source of spiritual education. It gives us access to the active intelligence of the universe and teaches us how to understand and heal our Earth.

The Nature of Sacred Space

The dimensions of a sacred space vary. It can occupy anything from the corner of a room to an altar, a Gothic cathedral, a mountain, the ocean, the planets, the solar system, the universe, or beyond. Sacred space is the microcosm of the macrocosm of our multiuniversal existence.

Sacred space in its natural form has existed on Earth since the creation of the planet. During the formation of the Earth, the minerals emerging from its core brought with them an electromagnetic charge. Springs carried this charge to the surface, lakes held the charged water, and rivers carried it to the oceans.

There is a grid of energy lines, known as the tetragrammation, that encircles and interpenetrates the physical Earth. Sacred space forms at the intersections along this grid.

Early human beings, often led by animals, discovered the locations of sacred space. They gathered in these places for fertility ceremonies and healing rituals. They built stone temples near or over them, defining these areas as sacred and separate from their worldly life. As differentiated religions developed, spiritual leaders chose these ancient sites for their temples and churches. Today, the most powerful places of worship throughout the world continue to cover and contain natural sacred space.

Natural Sacred Places

Springs, mountains, caves, groves of trees, single trees, rocks, rock formations, canyons, cliffs, rivers, lakes, deserts, oceans, hills, the Earth, the sky.

Manmade Sacred Places

Earth mounds, temples, churches, cathedrals, pagodas, wells, sanctuaries, stone circles, stone monuments, shrines, ceremonial cities, pyramids, chalk figures.

The Experience of Sacred Space

We are constantly interacting with space. Our senses perceive space as we relate to our physical environment. We see, hear, smell, feel, and taste space. As a result, it has a multifaceted effect on us.

We live in physical space from conception to death. Although we are not usually conscious of it, our physical space affects us deeply. We see a room as the area between walls. We hear the singing of birds outside. We smell turkey roasting in the kitchen. We feel the heaviness of the air when it is about to rain. We taste a delicious food even before it arrives in our mouths.

We also perceive space through our subtle senses with our inner vision, inner hearing, inner touch, and occasionally, inner smelling and tasting. The most common inner perception of space is through touch, or kinesthetic sensation. We "feel" the energy of a place.

A space may feel friendly and welcoming, or hostile and

rejecting. We may want to spend a long time in one place, and in another leave as quickly as possible. This intuitive feeling about a space has a real, concrete basis to it, due to the reality of the energy that collects there. We can use this intuitive sense of space as a guide and protector while meeting life's many challenges.

We each live in a personal energy envelope, known as our energy field. This cloudlike field of electromagnetic energy surrounds and interpenetrates our physical bodies. It forms a fine web of energy lines, which holds our physical bodies together in the same way the tetragrammation holds the Earth in place. This web contains highly sensitive, subtle nerves that carry messages to the physical nervous system. The content of these messages appears to us through dreams, thoughts, physical sensations, visions, and intuition.

Our energy fields are very sensitive to those of other people and of the spaces we inhabit. We move through life enveloped in this field of sensitivity, with our subtle nerve antennae continually reaching out to feel the quality of our environment.

When we feel physical or emotional pain, our energy fields contract in self-defense. Knots or blocks form along the pathways of our subtle nerves in response to these contractions. Chronic contractions lead to major blocks in the flow of our energy. These blocks are like dams in a river. If the blocks intensify, they may eventually lead to physical dysfunction or disease. Our energy fields hold the memory of past pain, and the fear of repeating these painful situations keeps the blocks in place. When we release the fear, we free the memory, and the blocks disappear.

We can identify a block in the physical body as a disease, dysfunction, or disability. Emotional blocks manifest as guilt, phobias, addictions, and fear. Mental blocks are reflected in disturbances and disorders of the mind.

Spiritual blocks express themselves in thoughts and emotions that obstruct our acceptance of spirit into our daily lives.

We come into life with some blocks already in place. We struggle, especially in the first half of life, to break through these blocks, which form perceptual networks known as karmic patterns. They influence our perception of ourselves and the world around us, and they govern the choices we make, until we become conscious of their destructive influence. When we release the blocks, we free ourselves to develop our full potential and our creativity.

The way we transform our karmic patterns is by confronting our fears and healing our pain. This we do best through love. As we release the blocks by opening our energy fields, we become more sensitive to sacred space. At the same time, we enhance the flow of love to and from ourselves.

The Healing Power of Sacred Space

Space records the vibrational frequency of all beings who have inhabited it. This recording is similar to an audiotape or videotape on which sounds or images have been imprinted.

Rocks, trees, soil, flowers, animals, and insects all express a vibrational frequency that becomes imprinted on the space they inhabit. The strongest vibrational influences are the thoughts and emotions of human beings.

The intensity of the electromagnetic energy in sacred places magnifies our experience of them. This energy is a powerful healing force. It functions as medicine for our energy fields, activating our natural self-healing capacities.

Although the effect is unique to each of us, general responses to the healing power of sacred space are as follows:

Physical

    Relaxes muscles and relieves tension
    Activates the immune system
    Stimulates sexual vitality and the endocrine system
    Increases circulation of the blood
    Opens nerve pathways

Emotional

    Creates peace and security
    Provides comfort and unconditional love
    Inspires feelings of belonging and oneness
    Releases pain and fear
    Relieves guilt and grief

Mental

    Releases painful memories
    Facilitates problem solving
    Transforms negative thought patterns
    Enhances decision-making capacities
    Awakens universal knowledge

Spiritual

    Facilitates telepathic communication
    Stimulates visionary power
    Facilitates healing by spirits
    Accentuates awareness of oneness
    Activates higher consciousness

Iguaçu Falls, Argentina

Temple of the Moon, Teotihuacán, Mexico

Chapter 2

THE EFFECT OF
SACRED SPACE

The effect that sacred space has on us depends on our ability to attune and connect to its power. Sacred space affects everyone who enters it, even those who are not consciously aware of its impact. However, if we approach sacred space intending to communicate and receive healing and knowledge from it, we will gain more from our experience. The effects can vary from aligning our inner personal center with the center of the universe to guiding us on an inner journey of self-exploration to accessing knowledge imprinted in the environment.

Cosmic Center

Space is an intermediary between chaos and the cosmos. When we sense the open-ended potential of space, we experience chaos. When we perceive order in space, we feel comfort and security.

Time orients us in space, providing a focal point through which to relate to our physical existence. We arrange our lives in linear time, planning for events. This works well for us, because we live in bodies that adhere to a linear course of birth, life, and death. If we were to follow the twenty-four hours of the day around in a circle, however, we would enter cyclical time, where there is no beginning and no end.

Sacred space exists in cyclical time. Here we lose our sense of linear time. The sensation of being in cyclical time attunes us to the natural rhythms of the universe in which time does not exist.

Cyclical spirals continually spin around a cosmic center. The cosmic center, too, is in constant motion, although with our limited consciousness we perceive it as a single point. What brings us to this dynamic cosmic center is the energy of sacred space. It takes us out of what we perceive to be the chaos of our lives, and reminds us that there is wisdom and order around and within us.

When entering a temple, house, or room, for example, we intuitively seek the center to orient ourselves. In the process, we may become aligned with the spiraling motion of the universe. Once we accept this spiraling universal force, we can move easily and peacefully through our lives.

Humanity has been in a state of resistance for many centuries. We have lived in linear time, identifying our reality with the course of our physical lives. As a result, we have tried to impose our will over the order of the universe rather than align it with the natural flow. This wasn't always so, however.

Ancient architects built temples over places on the Earth where they perceived the strongest electromagnetic energy. They began a temple's design with a central point in the place of highest energy. They then drew a circle around this point to initiate the building of the temple, and proceeded to create the structure around it. This sacred point represented the oneness of the original source—the cosmic center, where there is no beginning and no end.

The temples helped people locate the cosmic center so they could align with it more easily. They believed the cosmic center was the meeting place of heaven and Earth.

Epidaurus Theater, Epidaurus, Greece

Temple of Athena, Delphi, Greece

The Holy Grail

The Holy Grail is a sacred place where we find union with the divine in all its magnificent splendor. The quest for the Grail is the return journey to paradise and the cosmic center, which reflects our personal spiritual journey back to our own sacred center. This journey is an inner pilgrimage to find our connection to God. As a pilgrimage, it holds all the challenges, tests of faith, and encounters with fear and pain that are contained in the search for the Holy Grail.

Common symbols of the Holy Grail are a stone, a vase, a chalice (sometimes with a heart) or cup, the sacred heart of Jesus, a lance, a sword, an all-seeing eye, a downward-pointed triangle, and a holy book. When the quest for the Holy Grail is associated with a holy book, it acts as a guide in the search for the holy word. The holy word refers to the source of oneness from which all else has emerged. The "word" is sound. If no one listens, there is no sound. In the presence of a listener, however, oneness divides into multiplicity, resulting in both the sound and the listener.

The purpose of the Holy Grail is to bring us into the presence of the living God who dwells in each of our hearts. All forms of sacred space help us come close to the experience of this living God. Since the Divine Mother is the holy vessel who carries the spark of God, she is associated with both the Holy Grail and sacred space.

Sacred Stones

Stones consist of molten minerals that harden in the Earth's atmosphere. Since minerals are excellent conductors of energy, they are powerful channels for electromagnetic currents around the Earth.

Sacred stones acted as focal points for ancient religions. The Dome of the Rock, in Jerusalem, has been one of the most sacred places in the world for Jews, Christians, and Muslims.

The Kabaah, the stone from which Mohammed ascended to receive the laws of Islam, has been a holy site for Muslims. Moses received the Ten Commandments on a stone tablet. The Incas in South America focused their religion around the stones of sacred mountains. The Corn Rock marks the place of emergence for the Hopi people of northern Arizona.

Stone monuments and circles throughout Europe denote places that have been sacred to successive cultures for thousands of years. Ancient Greek priests and priestesses communicated with the spiritual world and with each other through Omphalos Stones. Oghaum Stones in Ireland energized healing and prophetic powers for the Druids. Today, passage mounds found in England, Ireland, and France contain mysteriously marked stones. A sacred stone still sits beneath the Coronation Chair at Westminster Abbey, in London, England. For centuries the goal of alchemy was to directly access the philosophers' stone. And as was mentioned earlier, one form of the Holy Grail is a sacred stone or stones.

My first experience with Grail Stones was at Chartres

Turoe Stone, Turoe, Ireland

Stone Goddess of Ggantija, Ggantija, Malta

Stone Goddess of Lombrives Cave, Ussat-les-Bains, France

Grand Menhir Brise Stone, Brittany, France

Entrance stone to Passage Mound, Newgrange, Ireland

Cathedral's Chapel of St. Anne, in Chartres, France. One cold January morning, I sat in the choir of the chapel with my tape recorder in hand, and I asked for a message from Divine Mother Mary. She told me that the Grail was buried under one of the windows in the cathedral. She described the Grail as a stone of yellow-green light that had demateri-alized from outer space, and said only people with inner sight could see it. At a certain point in our planetary development, she continued, this stone and others like it would materialize so that everyone could see them.

Later that day, I discovered several representations of the Grail in carvings on the north portals of the cathedral. One was of Melchizedek, who holds a chalice containing a Grail Stone. Another was of the Ark of the Covenant bearing a large Grail Stone.

In *Persival* the Grail is described as a green jewel called *lapis exillas*. *Lapis* is the Latin word for stone, and some people say that *exillas* is a variant of *ex caelis*, meaning "fallen from the sky." This information suggests that the Grail is "a stone fallen from the sky" and that what we think of as Grail Stones are pieces of it.

Chapel of St. Anne, Chartres Cathedral, Chartres, France

Melchizedek with Grail Cup, Chartres Cathedral, Chartres, France

Ark of the Covenant with Grail Stone, Chartres Cathedral, Chartres, France

According to myth, the purpose of the Grail is to show us that we *are* the Grail. The answer to the question "Who does the Grail serve?" is, it serves each one of us, for we are all expressions of God.

When we become sensitive to the energy of the Grail and other sacred stones, we can attune to their healing power and wisdom. Not all stones hold this power; only sacred ones have the capacity to channel powerful currents that open our energy fields so that we can receive more vital life force from the Earth. This vital force heals our physical and emotional bodies and activates our sexual energy.

For direct messages received from stones at major sacred sites around the world, see chapter 3.

Sacred Crystals

Large crystals are buried under many sacred sites around the world. Beings from other dimensions are said to have brought these crystals here aeons ago. They imprinted them with knowledge and power, then buried them deep in the Earth. The purpose of these crystals is to hold the Earth in balance by keeping it aligned with electromagnetic currents from other celestial bodies.

When the time is right, we will discover these sacred crystals. They, too, are Grail Stones. According to many explorers of ancient ceremonial sites, they will guide us in the next stages of our individual and planetary development.

Following are some of the proposed primary and secondary burial sites of sacred crystals. Although many other such sites are also said to exist, these lists are composed of places I have visited, so I can speak firsthand of the knowledge transmitted by their crystals.

Primary Crystal Burial Places
   Temple of the Sun, Machu Picchu, Peru
   Sucsayhuaman and Ollantaytambo, Cuzco, Peru
   Temple of Uxmal, Uxmal, Mexico
   Capilla del Cristo de la Luz, Toledo, Spain
   Mezquita, Córdoba, Spain
   Montserrat, Barcelona, Spain
   Chartres Cathedral, Chartres, France
   Carnac Stones, Carnac, France
   Mont-Saint-Michel, France
   Castle of Queribus, Cucugnan, France
   Temples of Tiahuanaco and Pukankara, Tiahuanaco,
      Bolivia
   Temple of Ggantija, Ggantija, Malta
   Mount Shasta, California, United States
   Sedona, Arizona, United States
   Delos Island and Delphi, Greece
   Dome of the Rock, Jerusalem
   Newgrange Passage Mound, Ireland
   Stonehenge, Avebury, and Glastonbury,
      England
   Great Pyramid of Giza and Temple of Luxor, Egypt

Secondary Crystal Burial Places
   Tulum, Teotihuacán, and Chichén Itzá, Yucatán, Mexico
   Gothic cathedrals, Europe
   Monségur, Aguilar, Peyrepertuse, Usson, Languedoc,
      France
   Major temples, Egypt
   Parthenon, Greece
   Church of the Holy Sepulchre, Jerusalem
   Chimayó Sanctuary, Chimayó, New Mexico, United
      States
   Mount Lopez, Bariloche, Argentina

Trompul, St. Martin de los Andes, Argentina
Stone monuments and passage mounds, Ireland,
    England, and France
Taulas, Island of Menorca, Spain

According to numerous reports, the activation of these sacred crystals will occur gradually over the next several hundred years. Some are *libraries* that hold information about advanced technologies, spiritual truths, agricultural innovations, cosmic interrelationships, and much more. Others are *communication stations* that send and receive light-coded information. Still others act as *stabilizing points*, holding the Earth on its axis and in its rotation around the sun. The functions of additional sacred crystals will no doubt come to light as time passes.

The Divine Mother

Prehistoric people around the world worshiped the Divine Mother, whom they considered to be the source of all creation. Hence, the power of sacred space derives not only from the energized stones and crystals it contains but also from the Divine Mother. Many ancient ceremonial sites have been dedicated to her in her various forms.

During my years of travel, I recorded messages not only from the spirits of sacred places but from my own spirit guides as well. My primary guide, as it turned out, was the Divine Mother Mary. Because I grew up in the Unitarian Church with no conscious belief in God, I was surprised when Mary came to me. Later, I realized that my religious education actually helped me to accept Mary as a guide, since I had no preconceived ideas of who she was or was not. She came to me for my own healing and the healing of others, and to help us balance the energy of the Earth. Her presence, also apparent to others, evoked an opening of the feminine for both men and women.

Parthenon, the Acropolis, Athens, Greece

Great Pyramid of Giza, Egypt

Gate of the Sun, Tiahuanaco, Bolivia

Chichén Itzá, Yucatán, Mexico

Castle of Queribus, Cucugnan, France

Taula, Island of Menorca, Spain

Although my name for the Divine Mother is Mary, she has many other names too, such as Demeter, Persephone, Astarte, Inanna, Isis, Athena, Aphrodite, Artemis, and Cybele. She is the spirit of the Earth and the Great Goddess. She is the angel of birth and the angel of death. She is a holy vessel, carrying the seed of life in her womb and holding the secret to spiritual power.

Chapter 3

THE WISDOM OF SACRED STONES AND CRYSTALS

M any sacred stones and crystals await our communion and communication with them. Brought by the ancient ones who came in light bodies to raise the consciousness on Earth, they have profound wisdom to reveal to us. Following are messages I received directly from stones and crystals in sacred sites I visited.

Oghaum Stones, Dingle, Ireland

"We are magic stones. You can wish and your wishes will come true. Consider your wishes in your heart. Ensure that what you wish for is truly what you want, for it will indeed come to pass.

"When the man of the human race understands that his role is to impregnate—to give birth through a woman and through the woman within him—and that there is a holy force of God passing through him, he will know that this is his to give, to share. He will heal the wounds of the past. What passes through him is gold: the gold vibration, the gold light, even the gold metal. Man impregnates woman with the golden word, bringing this seed to her. She receives it and gives birth to this golden seed, the seed of light, the golden word. First she holds it while it gestates in her womb; she protects it, nurtures it, brings it love. In this way, the love expands in the woman, and becomes the flower of golden love. The word is then set forth upon the Earth.

"I carry Christ consciousness within. I also carry the history of war—war in the name of superiority. I come now to speak so you can understand that the light was misguided for many years. War was fought for the Mother. All war is fought for the Mother. Humanity must learn now, before it is too late, that the Mother is present. There is no need to prove anything to her. There is no need to seduce her. There is no need to conquer her. I have been cooked in the kitchen of God. I come from a space and time that is close to the Central Sun. I have been brought here as medicine, a pill, awaiting consumption by those who wish to be healed and to be whole.

"In the one there are two. In your love for another, you can understand that there is one within the two. There is more than one for each of you. It is not that there is only one in the entire forcefield of the universe; no, there are three. Each lifetime you might find two spirit mates and one is dormant, or three spirit mates in one, or one spirit mate and two are dormant, or two spirit mates in one and one is dormant. The soul can divide into three, or it may stay in two, or divide into two and leave one part dormant. There are always three forces to the soul, and this experience will bring you into one."

Grail Stone, Chartres Cathedral, France

"Within the seed of the spirit is the elixir of love. Alchemists understood that the elixir of love is the dissolution of all experience of the self into one. For when you join with another, there is an extension of self into one. There is an augmentation beyond individual union—into the triad, the trinity, such that the one becomes two, the two become three, and the three become one.

"The Christ represents God in the human being and the force of love and truth, and in this way becomes the symbolic representation of the force of God. So it is that each being is coming into the light as the force of God. No longer do we need this world of yours to be focused on one figure, one apex of the pyramid. Now all will become one and you will form a circle. The triangle will dissolve into the circle, the square will maintain the force of the circle, and the triangle will be encapsulated within the square. So it is the prophecy of the future, when man becomes God and God becomes man, that the consciousness of all beings, as it was in the past, returns to the circle once again. As it evolves, it reaches a tension, the dynamic force of the three, that brings the circle into form—the circle of union, equality, completion, wholeness. For there is no other way."

Grail Stone, Ussat-les-Bains, France

"I hold the power to create electrical storms, electricity, and electric power plants similar to those in Atlantis. I have been in Atlantis. I was brought forth into this world long before Atlantis existed. I absorb electrical storms through my being, like a sponge. I can assist you in controlling the weather and the magnetic forces that move the waves and the winds.

"My substance is stone that was divided into many parts before the Atlantean period and before the Lumerian period. I can assist in the magnification time. If you wish to magnify time in harmony and comfort, you may attune to me. This will come more slowly or more rapidly, depending on what you wish. If you wish to have a child, I can bring the child immediately. If you wish to create a home, I can do so. If you wish to bring forth love, I can do so. If you wish to bring forth spirit in love, I can do so.

"The Temple of Solomon is in the heart. It is a place that holds love and electrical power. It is a power plant, similar to myself. The energy of dimension relates to the balance of electrical impulses. When the electrical force of the Earth is out of balance, there are storms and floods.

"The Temple of Solomon has existed for as long as the Earth has. Now the temple is moving to a new nonphysical place. Because of the Temple of Solomon, originally from before time, the Earth was able to remain in balance through the energies of the stars. The Earth could maintain its intimate and fine-tuned climate and equilibrium in relationship to the sun. The Temple of Solomon held in place the delicate balance of water.

"When you create and renew the Temple of Solomon in your heart, you move electrical current through the Earth. This assists the Earth in harmonizing and rebalancing. The Temple of Solomon is the energetic experience of love. Without love, the Earth weakens and loses its force, leading to the need for upheaval and renewal. As you replicate the Temple of Solomon, you assist in holding the balance and delicate harmony of the Earth tone.

"The Grail is the doctrine of love. Love is the essence and primordial force of the transmuted expression of God. Love is primordial matter. Love is guided, like a charioteer, by the mind, and opened, like a volcano, by the heart."

Grail Stone, Delos Island, Greece

"The Grail Stones will materialize in each place at a given moment, which has already been designated for this planet. The awakening will occur in about 2012 A.D. during the summer solstice. At that time the stones will come alive, assisting in the motion of the Earth and the realignment of

Earth's energies. In the stones there is a crystalline message. A radioactive material holds the energies of this message in a strong magnetic force—stronger than the normal magnetism you have on Earth.

"The dolphins are the messengers and they serve as tuning forks. When you attune to them, they release information. Some dolphins have been selected as primary teachers to the human race at this time. Presently, it is not easy for the dolphins to attune to the spirit world, for the pollution of sound and ocean is more dense than ever before and the chemicals more poisonous to their cells. Nevertheless, many dolphins have come to teach. You will recognize them when you look with your third eye. You will see on their heads something resembling a little winter cap with a tassel on the end. When you acknowledge them as teachers, they will acknowledge you."

Grail Stone, Cave of St. Baume, France

"The Grail is an energy sent from the star cluster of Alcyon through Arcturus, touching Sirius and the Pleiades then coming directly to spots on the Earth. Light beings came to Earth long ago in their travels through space. Upon their arrival, they recognized its delicate beauty and balance, as well as the richness of its natural resources. It was a paradise for them. Walking upon the Earth, they beheld it as a delicate pearl or jewel, and they planted the Grail Stones here to maintain its beauty, harmony, and position in the galaxy—a position that accords it a small yet vital role in the formation and operation of the galaxy. By releasing negativity, you can help bring forth the clear space needed for the Grail to manifest. At the same time, you will be helping to promote the delicate, intricate balance and equilibrium of the Earth.

"Objects in the material world now hold the force of the

Grail in place, containing it in geometric forms. If this force were released quickly, it would wreak tremendous upheaval and disturbance, resulting in huge electrical storms, earthquakes, and volcanoes. The Cup—one such object—symbolizes the holding of spirit in the material world. Now is the time for the Grail to be released slowly upon the Earth, assisting in the healing while enveloping it in a protective blanket of energy. The Grail is the force of true love."

Temple Crystals, Uxmal, Mexico

"There is a crystal buried beneath the Temple of the Jaguar. There is also a crystal buried beneath what is known as the Temple of the Magician. These two crystals hold the entire continent of North America in alignment with the constellation of the Great Bear. Each crystal—one representing a core male figure, and the other a core female figure—is valuable and honorable, and has a unique vibrational force. Both contain information concerning the nature of evolution and the cycles of evolution that have taken place over aeons of time. You are entering into the final birthing stages of a great epoch of discovery and transmutation. It will be of great significance to be present in the years ahead.

"During a period of approximately eighteen months beginning in June 1999, you will be drawn to many islands and other ancient places of worship. You will also be drawn to future places of worship.

"The Temple of the Jaguar represents the human body. Deep within the heart of the temple dwells the spirit who designed it. This crystal, as well as the one beneath the Temple of the Magician, comes from the Central Sun beyond the worlds. The Grail refers to this place as Camelot. In fact, sacred rocks everywhere in the world came from Camelot millions of years ago to bring Earth into conscious awareness of their home.

"The crystal in the Temple of the Jaguar is most similar

to the crystal within the Dome of the Rock in Jerusalem. Beneath these rocks there are caverns, and it is in these caverns that they dwell. The crystal in the Dome of the Rock was discovered by the Knights Templar and covered again so it would not be disturbed, and so it would hold its place in the Earth. Why? Because when these crystals *are* disturbed, they cause disturbances in the directional forces and electromagnetic energy of the Earth. It is important that this crystal remain here, for it is a doorway to the place of Zion.

"Earth has a strong magnetic force, especially within red rocks. These rocks hold a particular chemical and energetic activity that allows the knowledge and consciousness of the crystals to be known.

"The Atlanteans modeled their world on this knowledge, which came to them through meditations and through chemical ingestion. It is important to realize that the energies of Atlantis came from another design—another computer program, so to speak. The original source, the programmer of the programmer, was the consciousness known as Zion. It is also known as the Golden Light and as Armageddon. You may think Armageddon is a disaster, but actually it refers to the Golden Light state of creation. This information has been drastically distorted by those who wish to obstruct the transmission of such knowledge, which carries a great force of truth and hope. You might see it as the cart before the donkey: the image, the vision, once implanted in the human brain, will never leave. It will always be with you, and it offers a reality you have been seeking to bring forth for many lifetimes.

"The Temple of the Jaguar was modeled upon this image, although its construction was limited by the available materials and manpower. If in daylight you look carefully at the buildings, you will see other buildings that were implanted here by those who originally came to construct the City of Light.

"Deep within the Earth lies great wisdom. There is information about medicines, as well as healing with light and the mind. There is information about the stars and the planets, and about how they will shift during the next twelve years and over the next 1,200 years. These shifts will bring forth the blessings of love, truth, and wholeness.

"Each major temple site on the Yucatán Peninsula holds a similar library. Such libraries exist in many places on the Earth. The Mayan people were instruments of others who placed them here long before.

"These libraries hold information about the transmigration of souls and the nature of time and space. The substance of each message is oneness—the union of feminine and masculine in consciousness, body, mind, and spirit. If you wish to read material in the libraries, for now you can use light and sound. Between the years 2012 and 2020, the Earth will transform, at which point the stone beneath this temple will be revealed and understood."

Spirit of the Temple of Venus, Chichén Itzá, Mexico

"Venus brings the light of fertility. You can channel and magnify this light through instrumentation, your hands, crystals, and the light of the planet as reflected by the sun. The union of Venus and the sun, magnified and projected into the human body, creates life, as it does with plants and animals. The reason the light of Venus magnifies fertility is that it brings forth receptivity in the egg. The sperm, sensitive to such receptivity, will not even try to enter an egg that gives off poison or has a hard shell or an energetic force-field around it. Nor will the sperm enter the womb or vagina under rejecting circumstances. You can change the energetic forces of the egg, womb, and vagina through alignment with light and sound, and through the projection of love and truth.

"You will find egg-shaped figures in the center of these pyramids, which were brought by light beings many millions of years ago. They symbolize Venus, the egg, life, and union. You can now see how the energies of Venus, Earth, and other planets in the solar system assist union in bringing forth forms of creation; in fact, when life began on Earth, the sun, moon, and Venus were in direct alignment, which brought forth the spark of life.

"As Venus moves through its rotation, it activates patterns of consciousness on Earth. These come in the form of lines, crosses, squares, and small circles, one upon the other, similar to a bull's-eye. The shapes contain messages sent from cosmic bodies beyond Venus. Their light shines forth through these shapes into the consciousness of those who are sensitive to it and able to translate it into forms, words, buildings, and living systems. This is a time of awakening to the planet Venus as she enters her final stages of a 250,000-year return. She is coming close to the Earth, and hence her energy is more and more perceptible.

"You will find the longing for love increases, as it has each time she has come close to Earth, her soul sister. During the next 9,500 years, the energies of Venus will be impacting on the consciousness of Earth more strongly than they have at any time over the last 250,000 years.

"The windows of the Temple of Venus are aligned with these motions, even though the temple was not built to endure such a long passage of time. The knowledge was passed down through the priesthood from light beings who arrived here from Venus and planted an awareness of light-coded information and wisdom.

"If human consciousness could receive this information, there would be no war. There would be no countries. There would be only one world, one language, one people. Human consciousness does, however, carry the *potential* for this consciousness. It has been recorded in the DNA of your cells.

"The shape of this temple is not only fashioned as a seashell. It is also fashioned after the spiral that brings forth the information through the light of Venus. If you study the cellular structure of light, and look at the spiral shapes, you will see that within them there is coded information. It is in the form of a spiral because this shape reflects the ongoing memory of all that is, was, and will be."

Spirit of the Temple of Ixchel, Cozumel Island, Mexico

"Here you can see colored light strands that are made up of memory cells. The various colors represent the light rays that activate memory in your DNA coding. These DNA light strands, although inaccessible to present-day technology, form patterns. Their vibrational patterns are similar for souls that wish to join in love.

"There is even a memory cell for union with God. Its pattern, compared with those for the bonding of souls, carries a much larger force. Moreover, the strength of its vibration is eternal.

"The strands of light bond souls that move in parallel motion. Although they never touch, they move as if they were one. The priestesses at the Temple of Ixchel did not understand this patterning, but they did understand the importance of soul alignment for fertility to manifest in the body. When there were obstructions in fertility, they aligned the souls through their energy fields rather than through the DNA coding patterns."

Sacred stones and crystals offer us a vast resource of untapped power for enhancing life in the twenty-first century. This power is natural, available, plentiful, and safe. The technological advances and spiritual wisdom they hold can undoubtedly help shift us into the higher consciousness needed to save our planet.

The sacred stones and crystals await our communion. The key to opening the doors to their wisdom is our sincere love, respect, and desire to communicate. Ask and you will receive. Listen and you will hear. Give love and you will receive love.

Chapter 4

Attuning to Sacred Space

The vibrations of a sacred place originate from different sources within the space. Their effect on us is often personal and highly consistent with our state of consciousness at the time we pick up on them.

Thoughts and Emotions

Some vibrations of a sacred space emanate from the thoughts and emotions left behind by former visitors or occupants. In a place of worship, for example, we may feel traces of the prayers and the love of God, or Great Spirit, experienced by people before us. In a home, we can feel if the family life was peaceful and loving, or conflictual and isolating. When someone has died in a space, we can sense whether they died in peace and love or in fear and pain. When violence has occurred, especially a brutal slaying or a sacrifice, we may react with nausea and pain in our solar plexus. Even at the site of a centuries-old battleground we can feel the pain and suffering of dying soldiers and the trauma of warfare. We may also receive images of earlier events that took place there, including village activities and ancient ceremonies.

The first time I realized that space held memories was in Rome in 1989. When I walked into the Colosseum, I

The Colosseum, Rome, Italy

suddenly felt sad and frightened. I thought it was an emotional reaction to recent events in my life; however, the feeling grew stronger and I began to sense that these were not my emotions. Sitting on one of the stone benches above the arena, I closed my eyes and asked my inner voice for the cause of this feeling. Then with my third eye, I saw a vision of frightened men and women locked in caves and cages with crossed wooden bars. I cried as I felt the pain of one woman, calling out to the man she loved, who was being led away to the arena. I saw animals and people fighting with each other, and the animals eating the people. I continued to watch scenes of horror for about fifteen minutes. Although I knew about the treatment of early Christians at the Colosseum, I had no idea the space still held their pain and trauma. I cried for a long time, and then slowly made my way down into the pits under the building. As I looked into the empty caves, I felt slightly nauseous, but relieved and unafraid. Even now, the thought of this scene brings tears to my eyes.

Later that day, I visited St. Peter's Cathedral and experimented with sensing its energy. To my surprise, I felt strong emotions of love and joy in the square outside the church and very little emotion in the church itself. Upon reading the guidebook, I learned that the square was where people came to pray and listen to the Pope, and that commoners seldom entered the church itself, except on special occasions—all of which explained the variations in intensity I had felt.

Past-Life Recall

Although it can be difficult to discriminate between imagination and past-life experience, a strong indication of a personal memory is evidenced by a physical reaction. If a thought or perception is accompanied by a pronounced physical response, there is a good chance that we have recalled a past life. Our consciousness holds the memory of our soul's experiences, and when we are in a space that triggers this memory our bodies react. It is of course important to separate our personal memories from the thoughts and emotions of others who have preceded us—an ability that comes with self-knowledge and self-awareness, as is described below.

On the Greek Island of Kos, there is a large temple honoring Asclepius, the Greek god of healing. It was a place I had dreamed of visiting for many years. I was so strongly attracted to this Greek god that I had named my first healing center Asclepius: Center for Healing.

Arriving at the temple, I climbed the steps, feeling intense familiarily and also noticing a strange tension and discomfort in my back and stomach. I meditated in the living quarters of the priests, and asked for information about the meaning of my reaction. A vivid vision of the past came to me: I saw the temple crowded with men and women dressed in loose light-colored clothing, sitting and walking around the white structures. Small groups were gathered around teachers, who were speaking in different areas of the temple. Crowds of people were moving at various speeds up and down the steps, giving the impression of a place alive with hope and excitement. Climbing the steps, however, was a man in a white toga with his head down. I felt his defeat, hopelessness, and despair. Suddenly, a soldier grabbed his arm and pulled him down the steps. More soldiers came and arrested him. I realized that I had once been this man.

The meaning of this past life flashed into my mind. I was a philosopher who traveled to different places teaching the wisdom of the times, especially the principles of universal law and sacred geometry—truths that offered all people a way to spiritual enlightenment without intervention by the priesthood. I was aware that the leaders of Greece positioned themselves as gods superior to common people, and that I was threatening their authority.

As I watched the soldiers drag me away, my body shook with fear and nausea. My heart ached with discouragement and loss. I do not know what happened next, although I assume I was imprisoned, killed, or exiled.

This experience helped to explain my fear of speaking publicly about my spiritual beliefs. As for the discouragement, I could see that when we bring a past-life memory to consciousness, it can release emotions that have held us back from fully expressing our potential.

Past-life recall that results from attuning to sacred space is not always personal. At times we may sense the presence of someone else who is stuck in limbo between this world and the next. The cause of such an entrapment between worlds is usually a traumatic event or an unwillingness to let go of someone or something.

For example, I was walking near a cathedral in Vienna, Austria, in the mid-1980s, when I suddenly felt a sharp pain in my forehead. Since I seldom get headaches, I sat under a tree to meditate on the cause of the pain. Very soon I saw in my third eye a transparent figure of a man floating in space near a wall of the cathedral. As I continued to ask for understanding, I learned that he was a monk in love with a woman who had married another man. When the monk died, he could not let go of her, and even now, centuries after her death, his spirit remained in pain and longing. I sent him love and compassion from my heart, and asked that he be released to go on his way to the other side. Within minutes, his image had dissolved into the wall and my head had stopped aching.

A few years later, I was investigating places in which to hold a seminar in a town near Córdoba, Argentina. As I entered a small inn, my stomach became severely upset. I did not stop to ask myself what was causing this feeling;

instead, I left immediately, and later asked some townspeople what had happened in that house. They told me someone had been murdered there, and that currently people were performing black magic there. I thanked my stomach for insisting on a fast exit!

Another revealing journey into the past took place at Chartres Cathedral in Chartres, France. After finding a quiet place to meditate in the crypt below the altar, I saw a vivid image of a long procession of people. At the front were men who were carrying on their shoulders an illuminated stone on a platform supported by logs. They were marching in a spiral around a hill with a huge fire burning at the top. The men walked in a procession up and down the hill until the fire died, and then they placed the stone in the ashes. The stone glowed with a bright yellow-gold effervescent light, mysteriously giving off its own radiance, as if it were not of this world. The people showed such reverence and awe in its presence that I realized it was a Grail Stone, and that I was watching an event that long ago had taken place on the land where the cathedral now sits. I still shiver when I think of this experience.

An equally profound past-life experience occurred when I was in the Church of the Holy Sepulchre in Jerusalem. There a vision came to me of Jesus carrying the cross through streets teeming with people and animals. Hardly anyone paid attention to him, perhaps because the villagers were used to the sight of a criminal about to be crucified. A young girl, afraid and sad, I pushed my way through the crowd to follow the cross. I smelled the sweat of people and animals and heard the clatter of hooves, the shouts of vendors, and the jingle of chains. As I watched from a distant hilltop overlooking the throngs of people, I sobbed in despair. I knew I could not prevent what was about to happen, and I wondered what would become of us when Jesus died. Each time I remember this scene I cry.

Previously, I had had several past-life experiences about this time in history. The first occurred when a spiritualist minister placed his hands on my head in a church service and I saw Jesus walking up a hill very close to my home, which was below the street. The second event happened when I was in Rome at Easter, attending a reenactment of Jesus walking up the Way of the Cross on Good Friday. The Pope was carrying a representation of the cross up a hill near the Colosseum when I began to cry uncontrollably. I was overcome with sadness and grief for a man who was about to die for speaking the truth about love and the presence of God. I cried throughout the entire service as people in the crowd kept looking curiously at me.

I could not understand the depth of my pain, since I had little knowledge of Jesus' life and had never consciously believed in God. All I knew was that this event had touched something very deep inside me. It was later that I realized I had actually witnessed Jesus carrying the cross.

A similar physical reaction led me to a past-life memory while I was reading a book about the massacre of the Cathars in southern France in the 1200s. Coming upon a short passage about these people being burned alive and suffocating in a large cave, I began to cry hysterically, unaware of what had touched me so deeply. Reading on, I learned that the French monarchy and the Roman Catholic Church conspired to destroy the entire Cathar population because their belief in direct communication with God and equality of the sexes threatened the Church's authority. Years later, on the first trip Esteban and I took to the Pyrenees Mountains, I remembered the massive fires in the caves. My memory came clearly into consciousness while we were in Monségur Castle, where 200 Cathars were burned alive during the Inquisition. I could hear the soldiers down below, and feel the tremendous importance of remaining calm and centered in the face of death. I also felt the strength and courage we had while, clinging to our faith in God, we transcended the pain of the fire. The saddest part of this memory was recalling how difficult it was to explain to my ten-year-old daughter that she was about to die. I believe she perished without understanding the full meaning of our faith—a memory that still brings tears to my eyes.

Monségur Castle, Monségur, France

I later discovered that I lived in this part of France as the wife of the First Grand Master of the Templar, Hugh de Pagne. Initially, the idea seemed implausible to me and I wanted more proof. While sitting on the grass inside the ruins of a castle near Ussat-les-Bains, I asked for confirmation of this discovery. Closing my eyes, I began to meditate, but nothing happened. Then I opened my eyes and there before me I saw a woman in a long red dress with a train, trimmed in ermine, walking across the grass on the arm of a man. They were talking animatedly with each other and seemed very much in love. Feeling the joy and excitement of the woman, I took this image to be a picture of my life with Hugh.

As the couple walked past me, I heard a loud swishing overhead and looked up, somewhat fearfully. A large black raven was flying very close to my head—an event I recognized as a confirmation of my vision. In many cultures birds represent spirits, and they are attracted to the force of the electromagnetic energy of transdimensional communication; in fact, they use these currents to guide them in their migratory journeys. So it seemed that the raven was attracted to my transdimensional communication, validating for me the reality of this past life.

Electromagnetic Currents

Just as some vibrations of a sacred space originate in the thoughts and emotions remaining there, others come from the electromagnetic currents that run through that portion of the Earth. The Earth's electromagnetic currents are similar to the meridians of energy that acupuncturists stimulate in treating energetic imbalances.

Intersecting currents in the Earth form vortexes, many of which are located where minerals have erupted from the core of the Earth in earthquakes or volcanoes. Often situated on or near a fault, a vortex is an opening in the Earth's energy field, which allows for a free exchange of energy between its different levels. One way to visualize a vortex is to imagine a spiraling funnel of energy moving vertically between interconnecting horizontal planes.

Ancient cultures erected stone monuments and temples on the Earth's most powerful vortexes. These stone monuments act as "acupuncture needles," helping energy to flow smoothly and holding the Earth in balance. Among the most well-known of these are the ceremonial centers at Stonehenge and Avebury in England; the Carnac Stones of France; the Great Pyramid of Giza in Egypt; the Omphalos Stones of Greece; the Oghaum Stones of Ireland; and the

Carnac Stones, Carnac, France

stone temples of the pre-Inca people of Peru, Bolivia, and Ecuador.

For thousands of years, energy vortexes have been places of healing and fertility. Their forces stimulate the release of pain and fear, and magnifiy prophetic abilities. Because the spirit can more easily leave the body in places of high electromagnetic force, they have served as funerary and burial sites. The Celtic people, for instance, referred to the Carnac Stones as a resting place for heroes on their way to the Isle of the Blest.

In the ceremonial city of Machu Picchu, high in the Andes Mountains of Peru, Inca priests and priestesses communicated with the spirits of their mummified spiritual and secular leaders to obtain information from the "other side." Several times a year, the priests and priestesses removed the mummies from their sacred caves, paraded them around the city, and then propped them up on platforms throughout the city, to serve as intermediaries. They seemed to understand that the electromagnetic currents in Machu Picchu helped the dead cross the bridge between worlds.

Temple of the Condor, Machu Picchu, Peru

Ancient priests knew how to transfer knowledge to sacred space, imprinting it through sound and thought into the rocks. They called upon guardian spirits to protect this knowledge until humanity became responsible enough to use it wisely. We are currently entering a stage of evolution in which people who embody love and respect will be able to access this information.

One way to avail ourselves of the information is through the nerve endings in our feet. These sensitive receptors are equipped to record the vibrations of sacred space, stimulating our energy fields to attune to the frequencies that exist there—much like tuning to a specific radio or TV station. In this way, we telepathically obtain information from the consciousness imprinted in the rocks. Until then, they remain storehouses of hidden wisdom, waiting for us to unlock their secrets.

Chapter 5

SPIRITUAL EVOLUTION

The intense electromagnetic energy of sacred space gives us an opportunity to take big steps in our spiritual evolution. Its vibrational power opens our energy fields to receive more universal forces, which flow naturally into our areas of physical, emotional, mental, or spiritual contraction. The extent of our opening and healing, however, depends on our receptivity and willingness to change. What we must do is open our hearts and say, "Yes, I wish to learn, to grow, to open, to receive." This intention invites the spiritual power of a sacred space to fill us with compassion and love. For this reason, it is often associated with the Divine Mother.

Spiritual evolution, or moving from a lower to a higher plane of consciousness, entails a return to oneness. This state of oneness may be achieved through any number of paths that are amplified by the power of sacred space. Here are some of them.

Pilgrimage

A pilgrimage is a journey to a sacred place through unknown territory, in search of union with the divine. This quest may be an actual physical journey or an emotional one.

Along the way, we encounter challenges and obstacles that open us to new modes of perceiving ourselves and the world around us. Many times, our only recourse is to seek further connection with the divine in order to solve these dilemmas. We leave familiar comforts and supports behind as we venture forth, only to discover that on the road our usual coping mechanisms are virtually ineffective.

For one thing, a pilgrimage offers intense, compact lessons in intimacy and personal connection. We come face-to-face with both our desire for and our resistance to union. Interestingly, the fears that we have about spiritual union are the same fears we have in our intimate relationships. This means that once we are able to confront and work through fears of spiritual union on a pilgrimage, we will find it easier to live in intimate relationships.

Our fears of being exposed, violated, consumed, betrayed, controlled, imprisoned, or abandoned all play a role in our resistance to intimacy and union. We fear that surrendering to spirit will re-create painful situations. For example, if we fear loss of control in a love relationship, as a result of excessive parental manipulation in childhood, we may also fear loss of control in relationship with the spirit of a place. If we fear abandonment in an intimate relationship, as a result of emotional or physical neglect in childhood, we may also fear abandonment by the spiritual world and resist any sense of connection with it.

As pilgrims, our dreams and visions become vivid indicators of both the rewards and the perils of our quest. Their intensity forces us to revisit our inner demons and make peace with the past. As we sink into the depths of our consciousness, memories of this lifetime and past lifetimes rise to the surface. In response, our bodies become hypersensitive and, vulnerable to past pains, inclined to manifest strange and unusual symptoms.

Even before beginning our pilgrimage, we may create different forms of resistance to it. As the time of departure approaches, we may experience a lack of desire to go, or a

Mont-Saint-Michel, France

variety of obstacles. Our egos want things to stay the same, no matter how unpleasant or unsatisfying they may be. So often, it feels more comfortable to stay with what we know than to risk stepping into the unknown. Resistance and obstructions plagued a middle-aged man I know while planning his pilgrimage to Mont-Saint-Michel, a small island off the northwest coast of France, until he discovered that to risk growth leads to a rewarding outcome. "If we take the first step," he said months later, "God will do the rest." He was fascinated by the sense of ecstasy and personal well-being he had felt in the monastery there.

Similarly, one night in a hotel room in Arles, France, while on my way to the Cave of Mary Magdalen, I began shaking in fear and anger. Seeking an explanation for this strange reaction, I saw an image of a man cracking my head open with an ax in a small stone room of a castle. When I asked about the cause for this bludgeoning, my inner voice said that my brother had felt jealous and betrayed by me. I do not know if the death took place in Arles, but I do know

Cave of Mary Magdalen, St. Baume, France

Dome of the Rock, Jerusalem

that with this powerful memory release came great resistance to continuing my journey to the sacred cave dedicated to Mary Magdalen. Arriving there at last, I had a strong sense that I lived in that cave with Mother Mary and Mary Magdalen after the crucifixion of Jesus.

A pilgrimage opens us to inner messages. We become tender, vulnerable, soft, and receptive to the love and comfort of spiritual guidance. Our defenses dissolve and our hearts expand with love. We receive healing, revelations, spiritual power, and many other blessings. We feel the presence and embrace of the Great Mother. We discover inner strength and, step by step, learn to trust in God and in ourselves.

Arriving at our destination, we sense its electromagnetic energy currents pulsing through our nervous system, clearing the blocks that promote negative thinking and physical disease. We free up energy to create the life we truly want. Old patterns of behavior and thought fade away, while innovative solutions surge into our consciousness. Impasses dissolve and decisions become imbued with clarity. Painful memories pour out into the loving embrace of the site's spirits. And the veil hiding our destiny lifts, revealing paths to our life purpose. As one pilgrim to the Dome of the Rock in Jerusalem put it, "Guilt dissipates, forgiveness flows, and healing flourishes on all levels."

The call for spiritual pilgrimage comes from deep inside us. Often we do not heed this call immediately; in fact, years may pass before we actually set forth on an expedition. Once we do, however, the hunger for yet another one emerges. If instead we resist embarking on another pilgrimage for fear that our desire for them will become uncontrollable, we will feel a gnawing sense of frustration and unfulfillment. Anytime you feel this agitation, look closely, for you may be more prepared for a pilgrimage than you think you are!

For suggested pilgrimage sites, refer to the lists of primary and secondary crystal burial places on pages 21 and 22, or simply listen to the call of your soul.

Initiation

An initiation is a transition from a lower state of consciousness to a higher state through a ceremonial process. Typically, it unfolds in eight stages: journey, purification, entrance, descent, letting go, communion, emergence, and enlightenment. A person undergoing initiation descends into the darkness of the unknown and returns to normal consciousness strengthened, renewed, and enlightened.

We experience initiations both internally and externally. We pass through the two most powerful initiations at birth and death, and lesser transitions in the time between these events. Formal lesser initiations include christening or baptism, birthdays, graduations, marriage, childbirth, divorce, and retirement. Informal lesser initiations include our first step, our first word, the first day of school, public performances, work presentations, travel, moving, buying a car or home, an operation, and starting or leaving a job.

The author's ordination into the Sedona Church of the Living God

For thousands of years, people have chosen to conduct their initiation ceremonies in places with strong energy currents. The power of such sites activates the human energy field to receive support from the spirit world. Although this world is constantly with us, our limited perception can block our awareness of it, which restricts the ability of spirit beings to help us. When we ask for assistance in prayer or through conscious request, however, the spirit world acts immediately.

At certain points in our development, the spirit world honors us with an initiation ceremony to help us learn to love, honor, and respect ourselves as vessels of God's love. These initiations also encourage and support us in manifestating our soul's purpose. Currently, many of us feel our mission is to help bring light, healing, and love to the planet. To feel worthy and strong enough to assume this task, we pass through many challenges in early life. These challenges—all forms of lesser initiation—lead us to respect and trust God and ourselves, and they teach us to value love above all else.

Initiations give us a huge boost in our spiritual evolution.

Summer solstice 1997, Machu Picchu, Peru

An example for me was my ordination into the Sedona Church of the Living God, which took place in the conference room of a motel in Sedona, Arizona. Places in Peru, Ireland, Greece, and Egypt all served as important initiation sites on my personal pilgrimages.

Peru

The Inca ceremonial city of Machu Picchu is a popular place for spiritual initiation. Many people who make a spiritual pilgrimage to Machu Picchu find that their deeply embedded wounds open and heal before, during, and after their visit there. This powerful vortex of energy, discovered in 1911 by the American explorer Hiram Bingham, is known to have strong, direct, and very active electromagnetic forces.

As I meditated in Machu Picchu's Temple of the Condor, I communicated with the spirit of this place. It showed me how the ancient priests and priestesses mummified their leaders' bodies to keep the spirit close and available for consultation on a variety of issues. I felt that Atahualpa, an Inca king who was killed by the Spanish, knew intuitively about the invasion beforehand. In fact, so accustomed was he to listening to the voices of sacred objects that when he was given a Bible, he threw it to the ground because it did not speak to him.

While meditating, I was suddenly overcome with love and compassion for Atahualpa, who tried so hard to lead his people wisely yet years later was brutally betrayed by them. I knew him intimately. I could see him, together with other spirits, in an energy field above me. Then, to my surprise, he placed a crown of light on my head, whereupon I felt a strong stream of energy pass through my body.

Over the next several days, I was extremely vulnerable—verging on tears, angry, and hypersensitive to negativity. My energy field was so open, and I felt so close to Atahualpa and the last events of his life, that rage spewed forth from me at strange moments.

Eventually, I began to feel lighter, freer, and cleansed of a deep pain, convinced that my current fear of leadership originated, at least in part, in that lifetime. I am most grateful for this Machu Picchu initiation and for the healing it stimulated in my heart.

Ireland

In Ireland, it was the spirits of the Oghaum Stones that initiated me. Esteban and I, en route to a conference in Killarney, were exploring the Dingle Peninsula, where we came upon a hilltop cemetery dotted with ancient oval stones, each about three feet long. Many were inscribed with short lines in the ancient Oghaum language. We later learned that early Christians had moved them into their cemeteries because they knew the stones held special power.

One day at the conference, I felt lonely and decided to return on my own to the cemetery. As I stepped out of the car at the bottom of the hill, the remains of my breakfast erupted suddenly from my mouth. After this unexpected

Oghaum Stones, Dingle Peninsula, Ireland

purification, I walked slowly and uncertainly through a flock of skittish, bleating sheep to the cemetery.

The stones lay in a rough circle. Sitting on the closest one, I turned on my tape recorder and began to document messages from the spirits. Making my way around the circle, I sat or lay stomach-down on each stone, and recorded its message. They told me they were brother and sister stones from outer space, having been dematerialized and then rematerialized on Earth. Each one described a different spiritual law, and some emitted a warmth as I made physical contact with them. I felt the healing energy flow deep into my body. One stone impregnated me with a seed of golden light—a great gift. I wept in gratitude for the love and respect they each gave me. Returning to Killarney, I was still vulnerable but felt much stronger and more alive. To this day, I think of these stones as my spiritual brothers and sisters.

Greece

Another initiation took place at the Parthenon in Athens, Greece, as I sat in meditation early one spring morning. When I asked to connect to the spirit of the place, Athena came to speak to me. She said, "I am the warrior expression of the Divine Mother. I come to empower you in your warriorship and leadership." She placed a helmet of light on my head and added, "I will be with you, and you can call upon me for help. You are not alone. There are many in my world that are close to you." Later, in a moment of despair, I called on her. She gave me a sheaf of wheat and poured liquid down my throat from a small glass, and I felt her power flow into me.

The Temple of Eleusis in Greece was one of the most famous places of initiation in the ancient world. Every year thousands of people from Greece and beyond streamed into this site. Since revealing its initiation mysteries was punishable by death, few people today know what really happened there.

As I sat on one of the fallen columns in the ruins of this temple, I decided to ask for a vision of the initiation rite. I sensed that it was time to reveal these mysteries so that all people could know about them. I also felt safe and protected, because I knew in my heart that I was not violating the space or its spirits. I began by introducing myself and telling the spirits that I came with love and respect. I felt resistance on their part. Then I asked Mary, the Divine Mother, if she could help me, as long as knowing the secrets of Eleusis was not in violation of spiritual law. She agreed to assist.

As my inner vision began to reveal the rite, I saw myself in a dark curving tunnel lit by torches. While I walked through the tunnel, flames flickered on the damp stone walls. A procession of many people before and behind me passed in silence through the tunnel; I could hear the whisper of cloth rubbing against the walls. Eventually, the tunnel opened into a large candlelit hall. We walked around the hall in a circular formation until stopping at our designated places. Then we passed around a pot full of liquid that we each sipped from a ladle.

By this time, many people had crowded into the hall. A loud rhythmic chant filled the space. I soon felt the dark room begin to swirl, sending me into an unfocused state. A moment later, I lost consciousness. When I came to, I saw before me a bright golden light that grew larger and took on the form of a woman holding a thin pole in one hand and a round object in another. This shimmering golden light form of a woman was wearing a gown and had long, slightly curly hair. After standing in front of me for a few minutes, she faded back into the darkness. I don't know how much time passed before my long walk out of the great hall and into the night.

I believe this iniation in ancient Greece helped people heal their fear of death. It also served as a personal initiation for me in this lifetime, helping me to believe in the spirit world. To me, the golden goddess of Eleusis was a form of the Divine Mother Mary.

Knowledge of this initiation has since assisted me in helping souls cross over in death. After facilitating communication with the spirit of a dead or dying person, I ask if it would like me to accompany it to the other side. I also ask the spirit if it would like to meet Mary who, as a Great Goddess, helps souls in their crossing. If the spirit agrees, in my inner vision I take its hand and lead the way to Mary. She embraces the spirit with her unconditional love, then it passes through her to continue its journey.

When I am working with the spirit of someone who is still alive, we sometimes take an introductory trip to the other side. Then I say, "Now that you have crossed over and met Mary, you can go whenever you wish. There is nothing to fear. You have control over when you cross over. I leave you now with love and respect." Each time I feel the profundity of this experience, I am grateful for the initiation rite revealed to me at the Temple of Eleusis.

Egypt

While traveling in Egypt, I underwent a variety of powerful initiations. One occurred in the Temple of Luxor when the attending guard showed our group to a room without a roof near the inner sanctuary. Previously, I had learned that the ancient Egyptians, like the Inca people, used animal symbols to describe levels of consciousness. So as we sat on the yellow sandstone of the temple floor, I meditated on the first level of consciousness, represented by the serpent. Some group members near me scooted back, then someone screamed. My eyes flew open, and to my right I saw the tail of a very large snake disappearing under the wall of the temple! "Please tell us when you are about to meditate on the serpent," one of the group members later suggested.

I received an even stronger initiation in the Great Pyramid of Giza. While standing in the Queen's Chamber, I asked for a message from the spirits. The chamber was crowded, making it difficult to concentrate, but I was able to reach a quiet place inside myself in order to hear the message.

The spirit of the pyramid said: "You are now being initiated into the Temple of the Lion. This is a place in the spirit world for harmonizing and balancing male and female energies in order to attune to the divine source of all that is. You will help bring this balance of energy to the Earth."

A dense, powerful flow of energy entered my brain. I swayed in dizziness. Images of people in white clothes, illuminated by candlelight, filled my vision. Around them I saw lion heads and swirls and clouds of light. Way off in the distance I noticed two lions facing each other in front of a pillared temple. The imagery was interrupted by a guard ushering us out of the chamber so that other people could enter.

I later remembered that the lion is a symbol of Earth and of spirit incarnated on Earth. Often, a pair of lions guard a temple or sacred city. In Western society, where we have extended this idea to the secular world, we find pairs of lions at the entrance to large public buildings such as libraries, government offices, and palaces, as well as to private residences.

Just after my initiation in the Queen's Chamber, we climbed up the narrow passageway to the King's Chamber. There Esteban asked the guard to allow our group to meditate alone in the room for a few minutes. Some of us lay in the stone sarcophagus—the only object in the room. I felt strong vibrations coming from the sarcophagus. When it was time to go, I thanked the guard by putting my palms together at my chest and bowing to him, whereupon he began to cry and tremble. "When you bowed to me," he sobbed, "I felt a bolt of energy pass through me. My whole body is shaking." Esteban and I wrapped our arms around him to offer comfort and support. Apparently, the initiation I received in the Queen's Chamber and the vibrations of the sarcophagus had filled me with so much energy that when I opened my heart to the guard in gratitude, I transmitted powerful energy to him.

I later discovered that this was not a sarcophagus containing a pharaoh or high priest. It was instead a bed for the highest initiations of the Egyptian mystery schools. In fact, the entire pyramid was an initiation center.

Several months after my visit to the Queen's Chamber, I had a dream in which a voice told me that the union of two souls is symbolized by two lions. This message struck a chord of truth deep in my heart, reinforcing my intuitive sense that the purpose of the Temple of the Lions—which expresses the union of a man and woman in love—is to balance and unite male and female energies on the path of enlightenment on Earth.

These and other sacred places offer us a unique opportunity for spiritual initiation. In the past, such opportunities were granted only to the highest initiates in the ancient

Avenue of the Sphinxes, Temple of Luxor, Egypt

The author, the guard, and Esteban in the King's Chamber, Great Pyramid of Giza, Egypt

Obelisk, Temple of Karnak, Egypt

mystery schools, who would then transmit the spiritual knowledge to lower initiates. We are now entering a time when spiritual education is open to *all who seek it*. Hierarchy and exclusivity are dissolving in the wave of higher consciousness that is spreading around the world. Many people are waking up and asking for understanding of the deeper meaning of their lives and for a way to connect directly to God. How timely it is that sacred places are opening their doors to help in this search for spiritual understanding and personal empowerment.

Balancing Sexual Energy

Sacred places not only assist us in our spiritual evolution by serving as pilgrimage and initiation sites, but also help to harmonize and balance our inner male and female energies. All spiritual traditions speak of the universe originating in a state of oneness, from which emerged the duality of male and female, or masculine and feminine. Each time these two energies unite, they return to oneness—a state sometimes known as the sacred marriage or the Tao.

The closest we can come to this cosmic union in the physical world is the sexual union of man and woman. Mystics experience this oneness in visions of sexual union with a deity of the opposite sex. Most spiritual traditions refer to a divine spark of creation that arises in the union of God and Goddess and in the union of human and divine. In Hinduism it is the Kundalini rising through the body's chakras that creates this union.

The connection point between male and female expresses balance, harmony, and peace. When we bring our inner male and female energies into union with each other, we promote inner peace, which then radiates outward into the world.

Near Bath, in southern England, a giant male figure

named Cerne Abbas has been inscribed in chalk on a hill-side. He has an erect phallus and holds an upright club. Although no one knows who the artist is, an ancient belief attributes the form to beings from outer space.

When I attuned to the energy of Cerne Abbas, the spirit of the figure said: "I am a prophecy. When men stop forcing women into submission, and when women are honored and respected, the Earth will come into balance and harmony. At this point I will disappear, for I will have served my purpose."

A chalk figure appearing near Cerne Abbas is said to be a horse. To me, it looks like a dragon. The energy emanating from it is sensual, sexual, evocative, and peaceful, suggesting it may be a feminine counterpart to the giant on the nearby hill. Together, they seem to show us the way to inner and outer peace.

In the early mystery schools, the initiates took a strict vow of celibacy, and they worked hard to transmute their sexual energy into spiritual realization. Now, in our present stage of evolution, we can work *directly* with the balancing of male and female energies in our love relationships. Actually, the Tantric tradition of eastern Asia has long focused on sexual union as a means to spiritual enlightenment, but until recently this practice was kept secret in the monasteries and was not allowed to enter the public consciousness.

Utilizing sacred space to balance sexual energy can help us form cosmic union within ourselves and within our love relationships. Merging our masculine and feminine energies, according to many ancient teachings, is a potent path to spiritual evolution.

Cerne Abbas, near Bath, England

Chapter 6

UNIVERSAL ORDER

Sacred space replicates the order of the universe and activates within us the awareness that we are an integral part of a great, vast whole. It also reminds us that we are not—and never will be—alone.

Beauty is a reflection of this universal order. We find something beautiful because it touches our inner knowledge of the perfect order within us and around us in the natural world.

Universal order expresses itself as numbers, angles, proportions, colors, shapes, and the five elements. These material manifestations of universal principles mirror aspects of the cosmos.

Numbers

Numbers make up a sacred language that describes the laws of the universe. We can often "read" this language by counting particular features in a sacred space, such as windows, doors, steps, columns, upright stones, statues, or figures. Occasionally, numerals themselves are interwoven into a space.

Numbers convey universal spiritual truths, such as duality within unity, or the trinity of the masculine, feminine, and God. Often, numbers communicate the embodiment of spirit in life. In effect, they show us that there is inherent order in the universe and that we can trust the wisdom behind this order.

Numerical order reveals itself in our life cycle and the growth of our physical bodies, the growth of plants and animals, the change of seasons, the relationship and movement of the planets and stars, the shape and growth of crystals, and the harmonics of music. Numbers govern every aspect of our lives as templates of universal creation. For example, sound is composed of harmonic relationships, considered by many cultures to be the original expression of God manifesting into form.

Here are spiritual laws expressed by the numbers one through twelve. Included are the geometric forms and the symbols traditionally associated with each one.

One: The Law of One
In the beginning there is one.

Geometric forms
Circle; sphere; circles in circles; center point in a circle; single object; single object in the center of a circle; single step, window, or doorway.

Symbols
A rose, the sun, the center point, one eye, the sound "om."

Two: The Law of Duality
Diversity exists within unity.

Geometric forms
One or two lines; two forms in polar opposition; two identical forms; two steps, windows, doorways, columns, or lines; a masculine-and-feminine pair.

Symbols
Heaven and Earth; sun and moon; man and woman; a pair of animals, flowers, or sacred objects.

Three: The Law of Trinity
Trinity exists within unity.

Geometric forms

Triangle; three steps, windows, doorways, columns, or lines; a grouping of three forms; a pair of figures with another single form; a column in a circle; a triangle in a circle.

Symbols

Mother, father, son; male, female, God; Earth, spirit, human; Earth, sun, human; heaven, Earth, waters; three phases of the moon; a fleur-de-lis.

Four: The Law of Manifestation
Spirit manifests through form.

Geometric forms

Square; cube; cross; four steps, windows, doorways, columns, or lines; a grouping of four forms; four points.

Symbols

The Earth, humanity, four seasons, four directions, four stages of life, four quadrants of the clock.

Five: The Law of Regeneration
Form regenerates into form.

Geometric forms

Pentagon; five-pointed star; circle within a square; five steps, windows, doorways, columns, or lines; a grouping of five forms; five points.

Symbols

Human body, five senses, five elements, five-petaled flowers (rose, lily, vine), sacred mountain surrounded by four islands, five points of the cross, Venus, marriage.

Six: The Law of Creation
The union of opposites brings forth creation.

Geometric forms
Hexagram; six-pointed star, or Seal of Solomon; two
interlocking triangles; six steps, windows, doorways,
columns, or lines; a grouping of six forms; a pair of three
forms.

Symbols
Hermaphrodite, love, health, luck, beauty, six-rayed solar
wheel, six senses (seeing, hearing, touching, tasting,
smelling, intuiting), six days of creation.

Seven: The Law of Completion
The union of spirit and Earth completes the cycle of change.

Geometric forms
Three-sided pyramid (three triangles and a square);
triangle in a square, or square in a triangle; septogram;
seven steps, windows, doorways, columns, or lines; a
grouping of three and four forms; seven-pointed star.

Symbols
Seven rays of the rainbow, the Great Mother, seven major
planets, seven stars of the Pleiades, seven days of the
week, seven notes of the scale, seven-headed dragon,
Osiris, God as the seventh ray of creation, seven chakras.

Eight: The Law of Rebirth
Evolution brings forth a new cycle of change.

Geometric forms
Two interlocking circles; two squares; infinity sign;
octagon; spiral; eight steps, windows, doorways, columns,
or lines; a grouping of eight forms; two groups of four
forms; eight-pointed star.

Symbols

Two interlocking snakes of the caduceus, waters of baptism, the Goddess, four pairs of opposites, the square forming into the circle, good luck, Hermes, transformation.

Nine: The Law of the Whole
The cycle is complete and whole.

Geometric forms

Circle with nine points, or with eight points and one in the middle; a grouping of nine forms; enneagram; three groups of three forms; a grouping of four and five forms; square and pentagon; nine steps, windows, doorways, columns, or lines; nine-pointed star; two triangles in a third triangle.

Symbols

Earthly paradise; Triple Goddess; the limit of the cycle; three worlds of heaven, Earth, and hell; truth (when multiplied, it reproduces itself); initiation; eternity.

Ten: The Law of the Cosmos
The cycle returns to unity.

Geometric forms

Column and circle; ten steps, windows, doorways, columns, or lines; ten-pointed star; a grouping of ten forms; two groups of five forms, or five groups of two forms; two five-pointed stars.

Symbols

The Maypole, return to origin, Ten Commandments, the monad (the recommencement and infinite expansion of a series), Tree of Life, the letter *X* (perfection), universal order, universal law.

Eleven: The Law of Mastery or Transgression
A step beyond of the perfect cycle of ten.

Geometric forms

Ten forms plus one; eleven steps, windows, doorways, columns, or lines; a grouping of eleven forms; a grouping of five and six forms; pentagram and hexagram; twin spirals or steeples; twin forms.

Symbols

Ascending spiral cone, unicorn, reflecting pool of water, two eyes, mastery.

Twelve: The Law of the Cosmic Order
There is unity within duality and duality within unity.

Geometric Forms

Twelve-pointed star; circle with twelve points; twelve steps, windows, doorways, columns, or lines; a grouping of twelve forms; a group of four threes, three fours, two sixes, or six twos; squares and triangles; two hexagrams; two six-pointed stars.

Symbols

Twelve apostles, yearly cycle of twelve months, twelve grades in school, end of childhood, twelve Knights of the Round Table, twelve days of Christmas, twelve tribes of Israel, four trinities, clock.

Proportions

The most significant proportion in sacred space is the Golden Mean, or Golden Phi, which occurs naturally in human and plant growth. It is the ratio of 3:5. Because this proportion recapitulates natural growth patterns, it reminds us of universal order. When we are in touch with the realization that all of life carries this harmonious relation of parts to each other, we feel a sense of belonging and trust. This is the reason the Golden Mean has such a strong impact on us. Further, it lets us know the universe is holographic and that we and everything else share a common pattern with the whole.

To experience the effect of this aspect of universal order, we can draw a rectangle within a rectangle within a rectangle, *ad infinitum*, all with the same proportions. The resulting diagram tells us that we are the universe—the microcosm within the macrocosm—and the universe is us.

Angles

Angles send messages to us through geometric planes and patterns. A right angle gives us a feeling of solidity and control. Angles of less than 90° send a message of contraction, and angles of more than 90° evoke a perception of expansion.

Angles affect the flow of energy around them. Sharp angles activate our minds and our individualistic thinking. Corners and right angles collect energy, impeding its flow. Rounded corners and circular and oval shapes encourage us to relax and flow with the surrounding energy; they remind us of oneness and that we are all a part of the universal source.

Colors

Color is refracted light. This light carries encoded information deep into our subconscious memory. Because each color vibrates at a certain frequency, we respond to various colors in different ways. Below are some common color associations.

Black: Primordial darkness, fertile void, nonmanifest potential, mystery, womb of the Great Mother, death, evil, corruption, despair, the Dark Virgin, and the dark aspect of the

Great Mother. Depending on existing circumstances, black can stimulate comfort, security, hibernation, or escape from pain, depression, alienation, hostility, or aggression.

White: Undifferentiated and transcendent perfection; simplicity; illumination; chastity; surrender; holiness; and the cycle of life, death, and rebirth. White energizes lightness, clarity, transcendence, and purity.

Red: Life, fire, the sun, war, physical strength, anger, Mars, health, and the masculine principle. Red stimulates activity, intuition, passion, physical energy, and sexual excitement.

Orange: Fire, passion, luxury, love, happiness, Mercury, splendor, sexual attraction, and creativity. Orange galvanizes sexual vitality, creativity, familial bonding, and fertility.

Yellow: Intellect, rational thought, the sun, humility, faith, and intuition. Yellow invigorates mental clarity, logical thought, assertiveness, determination, nervous agitation, and perseverance.

Green: Love, money, abundance, paradise, the Earth, nature, jealousy, immortality, fairies, and the heart. Green stimulates passion, prosperity, bonding, compassion, empathy, understanding, and emotional balance.

Blue: Communication, truth, revelation, wisdom, loyalty, peace, prudence, Virgin Mary, Venus, and the feminine principle. Blue awakens compassion, hope, interaction, serenity, harmony, veracity, and unconditional love.

Purple: Royalty, pride, justice, sovereignty, humility, penitence, Jupiter, God. Purple stimulates nobility, majesty, achievement, and attunement to divine will.

Silver: The moon, the feminine principle, purification, virginity. Silver energizes receptivity, vulnerability, reflection, and appreciation of the feminine.

Gold: The sun, purity, illumination, divine power, enlightenment, immortality, glory, the masculine principle, and God
as pure light. Gold stimulates enlightened thought, purity of
intention, honor, holiness, and reverence.

Our attraction to different colors relates to the condition
of our auric field. When we are in need of healing and rebalancing, we seek out the color that is weakest in our aura. If
we feel agitated, we will be drawn to a calming color, such
as blue or green. If we feel physically weak, we will gravi-
tate to red, for strength and vitality. When we open deeply
to spirit, we seek out purple or white. Our color choices in
clothing, furniture, cars, homes, and jewelry express our
need for different vibrations of the light spectrum.

Shapes

Geometric forms reflect many principles of universal
order. These shapes have a direct effect on our consciousness, bypassing our intellect to reach deeply into our innate
knowledge of the universe.

Circle: Wholeness, completion, oneness, totality, belonging,
unity, God, the Great Mother, the Great Goddess, unmanifest reality, eternity.

The central point of the circle expresses the original
source, or cosmic center, which is infinite, with no beginning and no end. Energy forms a circle as it whirls around
its center of gravity, reminding us that all things in the universe begin with whirling energy. Hence the circle is the
universe, and its center the point of creation.

Line: Duality, opposites, division, path of life, passage of time, differentiation.

A horizontal line symbolizes the temporal, earthly, material world, whereas a vertical line stands for the spiritual world, the cosmic axis, and the bridge between worlds. A horizontal line expresses the feminine, and a vertical line the masculine; their place of intersection signifies sexual unity and the act of creation. A straight line is associated with directness, goal attainment, and an undeviating path of conduct. A wavy, undulating line suggests movement, water, energy, celestial bodies, and consciousness.

Triangle: Trinity; man, woman, and God; Earth, spirit, and human; mother, father, and child; sun, Earth, and human; sun, moon, and Earth; the threefold nature of the universe (creation, maintenance, and destruction); surface (first form that contains space to create a plane).

A triangle expresses the evolutionary movement of the two ends of a line as they move in dynamic tension outward toward individualism (masculine) and inward toward union (feminine). The law of the Holy Trinity, associated with the triangle, states that within one there are two and within two there is one.

Star of David: The downward-pointed triangle—the solar, masculine principle; life; penetrating phallus; fire; heat; passion. The upward-pointed triangle—the lunar, feminine principle; the material matrix; the primordial waters; the receptive yoni, or vagina; the Great Mother. The interlocking downward-pointed and upward-pointed triangles represent the masculine and the feminine in cosmic union.

Square: Manifestation (the triangle opening to include another line), spirit entering form, God manifest in creation, the Earth, earthly existence, the world of man, stability, honesty, solidity, permanence, fixation in one place.

A square expresses the creation of an earthly foundation into which spirit descends and from which it ascends.

Cross: Cosmic axis, union of Earth and spirit, communication between heaven and Earth, Tree of Life, dualism, union of opposites, spiritual union, union of the sexes, spirit uniting with matter, sacrifice, spiritual protection.

The cross was regarded as a symbol of sexual regeneration long before the birth of Christianity. The shape is reminiscent of the cosmic dance of masculine and feminine, continually coming together and separating.

Spiral: Vortex of energy, creative force, cycle of expansion in life and contraction in death, manifestation of energy in air, the primordial waters of creation, the course of the revolving planets, the sun, the moon, the rotation of the Earth around the sun, original creation.

The spiral epitomizes the movement of creative energy and the whirling of the original act of creation. Evolution moves in a spiral, circling back upon itself in gradual expansion and growth.

Rainbow: Transfiguration, a bridge between Earth and spirit, the celestial serpent or dragon of primal energy, the throne of the sky god, the Last Judgment.

The rainbow portrays the highest state of spiritual attainment before enlightenment, because it contains all the colors of the human energy field. In spiritual terms, the "pot of gold" at the end of the rainbow is enlightenment.

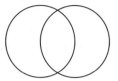

Vesica Pisces: Two interlocking circles, an upright oval or almond-shaped form, union of masculine and feminine, union of Earth and spirit, cosmic union, Christ as the fish, divinity, holiness, the sacred, the vulva, virginity, the Great Goddess, the Great Mother, oneness in duality, flame of spiritual enlightenment.

The Vesica Pisces expresses the notion that within two opposing forces there is always a point of union, harmony, and balance.

Elements

Five elements make up the basic ingredients of the material world, which includes our bodies and the environment in which we live. The elements hold specific energetic qualities that affect us at every moment. When the elements in our bodies and our environment are inharmonious and out of balance with one another, they promote tension, anxiety, and insecurity. When they are in harmony and balance, they foster physical and emotional health and help us feel peaceful, joyful, and secure in our surroundings.

The ever-changing nature of our bodies and the material world creates irregularity and inconsistency in elemental expression. However, when we add symbols of particular elements or the actual elements to a sacred space, they help promote harmony and balance. Their presence reminds us of the basic substance of the universe of which we are a part, thus bringing us into a state of connectedness with ourselves as well as our material and spiritual worlds.

Water

Qualities

Fluidity, the unconscious, primordial waters of creation, the feminine, the original source, change, the Great Mother, the Great Goddess, birth, fertility, liquid light, the unmanifest, purification, regeneration, rebirth.

Compatibility

Water and fire give us moisture and heat for life. When they unite, they form the burning water of life and the union of masculine (fire) and feminine (water), represented by Father Sky and Mother Earth. When they conflict, water extinguishes fire, and fire evaporates water. Water is more compatible with earth and air. However, excessive water with earth creates floods and excessive water with air destroys the breathing capacity of life. Conversely, an excessive amount of earth stops the flow of water, and too much air stirs the water into a storm.

The lower waters signify chaos, and the higher waters denote consciousness merging with the divine; respectively, these are associated with the lesser and greater mysteries. Water represents the dark, fertile void of the unconscious, through which we travel to find the light of the spirit, reminding us to flow with change and to trust in the fluidity of life.

Symbols

Circle or sphere, wavy lines, boats, rivers and streams, mist and steam, wells and springs, fountains, ice and snow, rain, fish, water lilies.

Ancient Sacred Space

Ancient cultures built their temples at or near a water source, usually a natural spring. The water from natural springs carries a strong electromagnetic charge from deep within the Earth, which facilitates healing, fertility, and spiritual insight. Temples were often built on riverbanks, seacoasts, and islands. Water is still used in sacred space for purification, baptism, and ritual bathing.

Personal Sacred Space

Vases or bowls of water, fountains, channels of water, fish tanks, pictures of water.

Chalice Well, Glastonbury, England

Garden of Alhambra, Granada, Spain

Lake Titicaca, Bolivia

Amazon River, Ecuador

Fire

Qualities

Transformation, purification, the life-giving regenerative force of the sun, the masculine principle, power, passion, consumption, heat, impregnation, protection, defense, sexual power, illumination, transcendence, inspiration and enlightenment, light.

Compatibility

Fire (active) and water (passive) coexist in dynamic tension. Fire and earth are compatible when in balance, but too much fire overheats earth (such as in a hot desert), and too much earth smothers fire. Fire and air are compatible when in balance, since fire needs air to burn, but too much air spreads uncontrollable wildfires and too much fire makes the air too hot for life to survive in it.

Symbols

Triangles, the phoenix, fire urns, flames, the sun, male figures, incense, fire gods, lights, candles, lanterns, the swastika, firecrackers.

Ancient Sacred Space

In ancient temples the light of the sun often represented fire and special attention was given to the sun's rays on the solstices and equinoxes. Fire ceremonies offered an opportunity to transmute negativity and purify the body, mind, and spirit. In many temples around the world, flames burn in a fire urn continually, day and night.

Personal Sacred Space

Candles, lanterns, incense, mirrors, a fire ceremony, a sweat lodge.

Crypt in the Abbey of Mont-Saint-Michel, France

Reflecting sun pools, Machu Picchu, Peru

Intihuatana sundial, Machu Picchu, Peru

Abbey of Mont-Saint-Michel (candlelit), France

Air

Qualities

Breath, life, light, flight, smell, thought, memory, speech, intellect, creation, freedom, the masculine principle.

Compatibility

Air is compatible with water and earth, but in conflict and dynamic tension with fire. Too much fire consumes air, and too much air blows out fire.

Symbols

Crescent moon, sailing ships, clouds, angels, birds, flying horses, winged animals, breath (*prana* or *chi*), feathers, bells, musical instruments, bowls.

Ancient Sacred Space

Air circulated through ancient temples via openings in the construction, such as windows or open-sided rooms or open roofs or arches, and in response to pyramidal shapes. The

Arch of the Nunnery, Temple of Uxmal, Uxmal, Mexico

Temple of Concord, Agrigento, Sicily

Arch at Castle of Ussat, Ussat-les-Bains, France

element of air was also enhanced by special locations, such as mountaintops or high platforms.

Personal Sacred Space

Skylights, special windows, open patios, paintings of sailing boats, birds and mountains, open archways and doorways, stained glass artwork, hanging plants, empty urns or crystal bowls, feathers, musical instruments.

Earth

Qualities

The Great Mother, Mother Earth, fertility, fecundity, resur-
rection, nourishment, creativity, matter, the physical body,
the feminine, solidity, reliability, material change.

Compatibility

Water nourishes earth, but excessive water washes earth
away. Fire heats earth, but in moderate amounts it burns
earth. Air purifies earth, yet too much air sweeps earth
away.

Symbols

Squares; figures of the Green Man; large cats such as tigers,
pumas, or lions; volcanos and earthquakes; mountain
stones, caves, and tunnels; valleys; flowers and vines; queen
bees; Earth Goddess.

Ancient Sacred Space

Ancient temples were built on or near sacred mountains,
caves, and stones to honor the element of earth, usually
aligned with images of the Great Mother in the natural
landscape. Gardens, trees, and pathways within or surrounding these sites honored the presence of earth. Figures
of the Great Mother presided over many temple sanctuaries.

Personal Sacred Space

Stones; plants; flowers; gardens; paintings of earth symbols;
forms and paintings of spirals; figures of the Great Mother
in any number of cultural manifestations, such as Isis,
Demeter, Astarte, Inanna, Aphrodite, Hera, Athena,
Artemis, Shakti, or Quan Yin.

Huayna Picchu, Machu Picchu, Peru

Kiva at Chimney Rock, Pagosa Springs, Colorado, United States

Earth spirit fresco on ancient palace wall; Knossos, Crete

Space

Sacred space, although it surrounds us every moment of our lives, is the least recognized element. Why? Because it is inaccessible to our physical senses. Only through our subtle senses do we become aware of its presence. Since this book is about the many characteristics of space and its impact on us, the subject matter is too vast to encapsulate here. Allow the two photographs that follow to awaken within you an understanding of universal order as expressed by the element of space.

Passage Mound, Knowth, Ireland

Owl Spires, Chimney Rock, Pagosa Springs, Colorado, United States

Chapter 7

SACRED GEOMETRY

Sacred geometry is an ageless treasure map to spiritual enlightenment. In sacred space it outlines numerous pathways to higher consciousness and spiritual truths. Often, clues to caches of hidden knowledge can be found in the overall formation of a space; other times, information appears more directly in features within the space. In either instance, the clues can lead us to troves of prized wisdom as long as we know how to decipher them.

Following are descriptions of the clues most often contained in sacred space, together with their effects on us. Always, sacred geometry activates intuitive wisdom that resides deep in our unconscious, reminding us of the oneness and beauty of our universal existence.

The Trinity

The trinity symbolizes different aspects of the Holy Trinity of One (or God), male, and female. The numbers three, twelve, and twenty-one, as well the circle, line, and triangle, are common geometric representations of the Holy Trinity in sacred space.

The Effect on Us

The trinity expresses the universal principle that we, in our male and female bodies, are part of one great whole and that we share this whole with one another. Experiencing the trinity gives us a feeling of belonging to something infinite, comprehensive, and whole. It tells us that we are not alone and separate—that we are simultaneously individualized in male and female bodies and bonded together in oneness.

Cosmic Union

Cosmic union, a reenactment of creation, is often depicted as a joining of male and female geometric forms through the merging of sexual organs. The male form is vertical, linear, phallic, and tubular, while the female form is horizontal, circular, and oval or elliptical.

Two-Headed Jaguar, Chichén Itzá, Yucatán, Mexico

The Effect on Us

The implication of sexual union activates our sexual energy and life force, so that when we perceive these symbols in sacred space we experience subtle pleasure and sensuality. At the same time, we touch our love of life and the beauty of male and female in love.

Meeting of Earth and Spirit

Sacred space is a place where Earth and spirit meet. The meeting point forms a cross where the vertical plane, represented by an upright stone, a column, or a steeple, intersects the horizontal plane, represented by a reclining stone, a circular platform, the flattened top of a hill, or a flat horizon. The vertical plane channels the ascent and descent of spirit, whereas the horizontal one receives spirit and transmutes it into matter. So it is that a vertical line expresses a pathway to the sky, a horizontal line symbolizes spirit on Earth, and their point of intersection portrays the union of spirit and Earth.

The Effect on Us

The meeting of heaven and Earth reminds us that we are containers and expressions of spirit, and that we exist in spirit as well as matter. The point of intersection amplifies our consciousness of cosmic union and our awareness that we exist in both oneness and duality.

Secret Sanctuary

A sacred space often has at its center a secret sanctuary which, hidden from public view, represents the hub of spiritual power. This primary energy source is usually marked by an altar, a tone, a circle of stones, a design on the floor, light through a window, steps, a pyramid, or a circular form. It may be underground or in an enclosure or a cave. The secret sanctuary is the "Holy of Holies," the place of power, and the inner sanctum. It symbolizes the womb of the Great Mother, where cosmic union gives forth to creation. The passageway leading to and from the sanctuary represents the vagina and birth canal.

Temple of the Moon, Teotihuacán, Mexico

Stone circle, Cornwall, England

Mihrab, Mezquita, Córdoba, Spain

The Effect on Us

Secret sanctuaries are exciting, mysterious, and evocative. We are intuitively attracted to them, because we sense that they contain a precious treasure. Surmounting the barriers we encounter on our journey to them further enhances their value. Dark concealed places arouse our sexual energy and remind us of the pleasures of union. Here we remember the dark, fertile womb of the Great Mother from whom we came and to whom we shall return, giving rise to a sense of belonging and mystery.

Sacred Mountain

A mountain is symbolic of spiritual ascension and spiritual evolution. We often find sacred places at the tops of mountains and in high altitudes. Symbols of the sacred mountain are ascending stairs, a pyramid, a triangle, trapezoidal windows and doorways, and the view of a sacred mountain from a window. Mountains attract us because of both the power of their energy and our intuitive awareness of our capacity to ascend to spirit.

Pyramid of the Magician, Temple of Uxmal, Uxmal, Mexico

The Effect on Us

Sacred mountains draw us upward toward inspiration and higher consciousness. The peak of a sacred mountain reminds us that our goals are achievable and real. While climbing, we feel the Earth's power to manifest a magnificent mountain that reaches into the heavens. The solidity of the mountain suggests continuity and permanence, offering us reassurance and comfort in a rapidly changing world.

Orientation to the Stars

Sacred space is usually oriented toward the sun, our closest star, and more subtly, the polar star, Polaris, or a constellation or planet. Traditionally, the entrance to a sacred place faces the rising sun to the east, where it receives the light of new beginnings and fresh life. Sacred burial places tend to face the setting sun to the west, which represents endings, death, and the dark, fertile void from which life emerges. Often, special stones or carvings mark where the sun touches the Earth at the solstices and equinoxes, charting the movement of the sun and the passage of time.

Temple of Venus, Chichén Itzá, Yucatán, Mexico

The Effect on Us

When we are oriented in time and space, we feel secure, for we know we are part of the innate order of the universe. In becoming conscious of where we stand in the great universal whole, we are comforted by the cycle of life, death, and rebirth. The reassuring emergence of the sun each day gives us a sense of continuity, and the sunset helps us let go of the old and make way for the new.

Burial Places

The strong electromagnetic currents that pass through sacred space ease the soul's separation from the body at death. They also invigorate the ascension of consciousness and its acceptance of the spiritual world. Ancient cultures knew how to activate and utilize this energy to help guide dying people, often transporting them across long distances to be in these places. Today, we bury our dead near churches and temples, some of which still contain high-energy currents.

In the past, priests and priestesses performed sacrifices in sacred burial places, perhaps to magnify their power or appease the spirits of the dead. Such sacrificial activities were a violation of sacred space; in fact, whenever life is taken in places that honor and respect generativity, the energy there becomes disturbed and the spirits suffer.

Burial places contain a variety of geometric forms. The most common are vertical and pyramidal, symbolizing ascendance of the soul at death. Here stones function as channels of energy to assist the soul in separating from the body and to hold the space for its departure.

Dolmen, Northern Portugal

Pyramid of Saqqara, Cairo, Egypt

The Effect on Us

The effect of burial places varies according to the soul-release rituals once performed in them. Those in which souls were free to depart convey a light, joyful, liberating feeling. Burial places that entrapped souls evoke a sense of doom, fear, and suffering. In a place of battle or natural disaster, where many people died violently, this sensation can be strong enough to cause dizziness or nausea.

Chapter 8

LIVING IN SACRED SPACE

Ancient cultures around the world lived in constant spiritual awareness. They designed their living quarters, body adornments, even their cooking utensils to reflect the beauty and order of the sacred world. We, too, can remain conscious of spiritual realities in our day-to-day lives. Inspired by our long-ago forebears, we can incorporate sacred design into a corner of our home or office, and into the jewelry we wear, the toys we give our children, and the clothing we dress in. After designing a personal sacred space, it is important to honor it and keep it clean so that it will forever remind us that we are part of a universal order based on love, peace, balance, and harmony.

Designing a Personal Sacred Space

A personal sacred space that reflects universal order and truth affects us positively, and we find it beautiful. Space that is chaotic and inharmonious promotes feelings of discomfort and insecurity. We find sacred design beautiful because it reminds us that we are an integral part of a beautiful world. When we perceive something beautiful, we feel uplifted, for it stimulates our consciousness to vibrate at a higher frequency. The higher the frequency, the more love and joy we experience and express. Ultimately, sacred design stimulates us to reach a state of unconditional and all-encompassing love, which is the formative substance of the universe.

When we surround ourselves with sacred design, our souls feel at home and at peace, no matter how much turmoil we may encounter in the outer world. The holographic messages of sacred design tell us that we are not alone and separate; we are a part of everything, and everything is a part of us; we are one. This is sacred living.

The design of any personal sacred space will depend on available materials, climate, interests of household members, spiritual orientation, and culture. Your sacred space might be anything from a small table or a corner of a room or closet, to an entire room, your whole house or office, your garden, a tree, a stone, or your car. Once you have chosen your site, be sure to keep in mind the following principles of sacred design.

Architecture

Doors and doorways provide a bridge between the sanctified and profane worlds, preparing us to enter a sacred place and reflect the energy it holds.

Windows and doorways frame memorable scenes that uplift our consciousness.

Steps guide us from one dimension to another.

Fountains remind us of the primordial waters from which we came, and express qualities inherent in the element of water.

Outer walls and fences define the perimeter of sacred space, protecting it from profane influences.

Geometric forms painted on doors, windows, walls, gardens, or hallways express spiritual truths.

Altars or inner sanctuaries mark the Holy of Holies, the sacred center.

The central point of a space represents the origin of the cosmos.

Circular and spiral forms create unity and harmony.

Alignment with the motion of the sun, moon, planets, and stars orients the space to the cosmos.

Gardens planted in sacred geometric shapes remind us of universal order.

Walkways leading to sacred gardens, patios, or sanctuaries are initiatory paths to cosmic union.

Natural materials carry vibrations of the natural world.

Reflective windows integrate indoor and outdoor space.

Water running in a channel, pool, or fountain evokes a feeling of peace and belonging.

Furnishings

Sacred geometric forms in furniture, fabrics, carpets, art objects, and paintings convey spiritual truths.

Colors vibrate at different frequencies and hence affect our consciousness in different ways.

Mirrors channel energetic flow and integrate indoor and outdoor space.

Indoor fountains promote a feeling of peace and oneness.

Art objects made of natural materials carry the vibration of nature into indoor space.

Colored glass stimulates a variety of healing responses.

Sensuous materials bring pleasure to our senses.

Objects that reflect the presence of stars, planets, and our moon and sun expand our consciousness.

Objects and furniture placed in geometric alignment with sacred indoor or outdoor space takes on a magnified presence.

Gold, silver, copper, and brass objects carry the vibration of these minerals into the space.

A table or altar, covered with a beautiful cloth, evokes reverence for cherished objects.

Candles bring natural light to darkness, reminding us of the radiance that can banish pain and fear.

Round, oval, and elliptical objects awaken memories of oneness, wholeness, and the source of love and life.

Live flowers and plants spark vitality; dried or silk flowers are effective subsititutes.

Rounded shapes both ease the flow of energy and create a sense of welcome and belonging.

Triangular or rounded shapes placed in corners facilitate the flow of energy through a room.

Thoughtful placement of technological equipment neutralizes its electromagnetic vibrations.

Soft spiritual music uplifts any space.

Soft lighting enhances intimacy and feelings of peace.

Lamps, lampshades, and lighting fixtures of natural materials counter the negative effects of artificial light.

Tapestries and fabric on walls and ceilings soften sound and light, creating an atmosphere of comfort and security.

Jewelry

Sacred designs express spiritual truths.

Metals, crystals, and gems channel energy from higher dimensions, affecting the consciousness of both wearer and observer.

Gold and silver vibrate at a high frequency.

Sacred geometric patterns and ancient symbols represent spiritual realities.

Loved jewelry holds the vibration of love.

Jewelry given in love reflects this love.

Our attraction to particular metals, gems, and shapes changes as we change.

Toys

Sacred geometric designs attract children, because they intuitively know their value and meaning.

Colors have a strong emotional effect on children, since their energy fields are open and sensitive.

Angelic music incorporated into toys awakens children's awareness of the spiritual world around them.

Interactive toys bearing sacred geometric designs help children integrate their earthly experiences with their memories of the spiritual world.

Round or oval toys remind children of the protective safety of the womb and the oneness of all of life.

Stuffed animals, often seen by them as alive, become friends, confidants, protectors, advisors, and comforters.

Toys resembling the sun, moon, stars, or planets remind children of their connection to the universe.

Fairies, gnomes, and fantasy characters heighten children's awareness of the elemental world.

Clothing

Natural fabrics, especially cotton and silk, vibrate at a high frequency and allow healing energy to easily pass through them.

Sacred geometric or ancient spiritual designs raise the vibrations of both wearer and observer.

Sacred robes worn in sacred space define spiritual intention and carry the thought patterns of meditation, prayer, and other spiritual practices.

Colors vibrate at diverse frequencies and thus affect the wearer and the observer differently.

Clothes influence the energy field around the wearer, through the fabric's origin, texture, shape, and color.

Sacred Objects

Sacred objects remind us that we are sacred and our world is sacred.

Sculptures, paintings, and photographs of gods and goddesses from around the world demonstrate the universality of spirit.

Crystals and stones from sacred places give off positive vibrations.

Geometric forms symbolize spiritual truths.

Handcrafted objects carry the vibration of their creator.

Objects of art express the artist's perception of beauty and spirit.

Natural objects hold the vibration of the material they are made of, such as clay, wood, stone, flowers, plants, rocks, leaves, horns, bones, earth, grasses, feathers, or seeds.

Maintaining the Power of Your Sacred Space

After you have designed your sacred space, keep it resonating with the love vibration of your soul. Be mindful of the activities you conduct in this space. Actions likely to maintain its sanctity and to keep the channels of energy open include the following:

Chanting
Prayer
Meditation
Singing
Dancing
Teaching
Loving
Initiating
Stretching
Celebrating

It is important to keep the space fresh and clean. To clean sacred space:

- Dust and wash it with love and respect.
- Scent it with incense, essential oils, or flowers.
- Remove your shoes before entering.
- Replace dead plants or flowers.
- Allow in plenty of fresh air.
- Burn sage or cedar to clear out negative energy.

Transforming Negative Space

When we enter a positive energy field, we seek to attune to its vibration. When we enter a negative energy field, we react in aversion and contract in self-protection. The message we receive from a negative field is that this is a hostile place. It may contain strong negativity, such as violent, aggressive, or painful thought patterns and spiritual forces; or it may hold the dense energy of depression, jealousy, or fear.

When you realize you have entered a negative space, leave immediately if you can. There is no reason to subject yourself to the downward spiral of negative energy unless important circumstances require you to remain there.

Any time you discover that currents of negativity have permeated your sacred space, transform it. This takes courage, determination, and concentration. Here are some methods to try:

- Burn sandalwood incense, sage, or cedar.
- Play drums, bells, gongs, or spiritual music.
- Ask for help in meditation or prayer.
- Perform rituals with white candles.
- Chant.
- Install sacred objects.
- Renovate the space by incorporating sacred design principles.

If you have recently moved into a negative space, remember that furnishings hold the thoughts and emotions of former inhabitants. If the situation demands that you stay there, give away, throw away, or sell everything that does not feel comfortable to you, and employ the purification methods listed above. Realize that you have the power to remove this negativity and to create a sacred space that reflects the beauty in your soul.

Chapter 9

COMMUNICATING
WITH SPIRITS

Sacred space, both natural and designed, is alive with the presence of spirits. Here is a way to communicate with them. You may want to record this exercise, and play it back while performing the steps.

Close your eyes.

Imagine sensitive antennae around your body. Extend these antennae into the sacred space. Expand the boundaries of your skin into the space. Notice what you feel physically, emotionally, mentally, and spiritually.

Say a silent prayer, such as, "I pray that this communication will be for the best and highest good for all involved here."

Silently introduce yourself, as you would to a person, by saying, "I am [your name] and I come with love and respect." Feel this love and respect in your heart.

Wait. Relax. Stay open.

Soon you will feel a sense of being lifted and expanded. (You are raising your vibration to meet a spirit that is inviting you to communicate.)

Relax and fill your heart with trust. (Your trust is the monitor spirits use to determine how much to open to you. If you try to control or force the communication, they will withdraw.)

Let yourself feel the love and welcoming energy of the spirit.

Repeat, "I come with love and respect."

When you feel you have made a connection, ask the spirit if it has a message for you.

Listen for the answer. You may think you are imagining the words you hear or the images you receive or the sensations you feel. This is fine, because it is only through your imagination that the spirit world can speak to you.

Relax. Receive. Honor. Trust.

Continue your dialogue with the spirit, asking whatever you wish—as long as it is respectful and honest—and listening to the answers.

When your dialogue feels complete, thank the spirit.

Say good-bye, letting your heart express gratitude.

Open your eyes and depart in silence, with love and respect.

After your communication with a spirit, you may feel disoriented, vulnerable, and highly sensitive. Know that your heart is open because of the love and camaraderie you received. Drink water, rest, and enjoy the blessing of love. Avoid conflict and stressful situations. Give and receive hugs. Write about your experience.

Communicating with the spirits of a sacred space can change your life. It can even change the world.

About the Author

Carolyn E. Cobelo, MSW, is a spiritual teacher and a leader of spiritual pilgrimages to sacred places around the world. An ordained minister in the Church of the Living God, she has practiced spiritual psychology for twenty-five years. Her extensive personal experience in passing through major life transitions assists her in creating deeply moving ceremonies and celebrations.

Founder of the School of Akashic Evolution in New York and in Buenos Aires, Argentina, Carolyn has taught seminars in North and South America, Europe, and the Middle East. She is presently the director of Akasha Institute in Santa Fe, New Mexico, as well as an artist, designer, and mother of three children. Her published works include *The Spring of Hope: Messages from Mary*; *Awakening to Soul Love: Pathways to Intimacy*; *Twenty-Five Power Places: A Travel Guide*; and *Avalon: The Temple of Connection*, a board game.